Let Us Imagine Her Name

Other Books by Sue Walker

Traveling My Shadow

The Appearance of Green

Sue Walker: Greatest Hits, 1982–2002

Blood Must Bear Your Name

It's Good Weather For Fudge

In The Realm of Rivers

Faulkner Suite

She Said

How Stubborned Words Mule, How They Balk & Take Their Own Measure

The Ecological Poetics Of James Dickey

Let Us Imagine Her Name

Sue Walker

Clemson University Press

ISBN 978-1-942954-46-0

Published by Clemson University Press in Clemson, South Carolina

Editorial Assistants: Ciara Marshall and Valerie Smith

Cover design by Ciara Marshall

To order copies, please contact:
Clemson University Press, 801 Strode Tower,
Clemson University, Clemson, SC 29634-0522
or order through our website at
www.clemson.edu/press/

Contents

Acknowledgments

I am grateful for *Silver Blade* magazine, who published *Nature Like Mother Is An Improper Name,* and nominated it for a Pushcart prize.

"The name: What does one call thus? What does one understand under the name of name? And what occurs when one gives a name? What does one give then?"

—Jacques Derrida, *On The Name*

"Give me a name? But why? I don't know exactly: maybe to lose my own."

—Jacques Derrida, *Parages*

[Pre]View

"I am because I say/I say myself/I am my name/My name is not my name/It is the name of what I say./My name is what I said/I alone say./I am my name./My name is not my name/My name is the name..."

—Laura Riding

And yet...

"In the joy of naming, one lives authentically. No matter whether I give a name to, or hear the name of, a strange bird; no matter whether I write or read a line of great poetry or understand a scientific hypothesis, I thereby exist authentically as a namer or a hearer, as an I or a Thou—and in either case as a co-celebrant of what is."

—Walker Percy

Since:

"The first step to wisdom...is getting things by their right names."

—E. O. Wilson, *Consilience*

So:

"Poetry names. If there is one thing it does, it is to name. It imposes identity. And it must name with words."

—Josephine Jacobson

Yet:

...names penetrate the core of our being and are a form of poetry, storytelling, magic, and compressed history.

—Justin Kaplan, *The Language of Names*

Therefore:

"I was you—you will be me."

—Anna Kamienska

A Prolegomenon or Preamble

in which she introduces herself, tells of herself before she knew herself, and considers coming revelations. She never knew her mother; she never knew her father, and was given away, perhaps sold, when she was born. A couple came to get her from there; there was a there there somewhere in Tuscaloosa. The couple kept her for nearly a year when someone said they knew the child did not belong with that couple. They said they knew who the mother was—and she was subsequently called into court. She said, "yes," she had given birth to this baby—but could not keep her. The judge then removed the child from the couple who had no legal right to her. He said the child's right was to grow up free from gossip, from the present scandal and he sent her to a foster home in Montgomery, Alabama. It was from there that she was adopted by a loving mother and father in Foley, Alabama where she grew up and became a teacher and a writer. This book, then, is memoir. It is discovery, the story of a woman who long wrestled with identity, who sought to know her history. Often she asked herself who she might be if she could be anyone, if she might give herself a name, and so this account is her own invention, a memoir in the form of an abecedarian—an alphabetical listing—whereby the writer makes determinations about who she might be. It is a hybrid work that indulges in forms variously dictated by the personalities involved.

In the beginning, however, there is history—two poems that imagine her beginning, and these poems serve as a sort-of prologue to the abecedarian that follows. Memoir is mingled with fact and fiction; it is truth and consequence. It is a conjoined work, an index or to borrow from Marianne Moore, a series of "conversities," in which the conjured personalities converse—or get to have a say in their own voice, a two-part presentation somewhat in the vein of Karla Kelsey's *A Conjoined Book.* In all, this memoir asks "What's in a name?"—and then declares how this means.

Furthermore, Moreover, Besides

Dean Young, in *The Art of Recklessness: Poetry as Assertive Force and Contradiction* says: "Poetry is yeasty proof of human life, record, and creation." This creation is a mix of prose poetry and lyric essay that ventures into various modes of telling.

Some poems make use of terms and forms specific to the person noted in the poem: the first poem's title tells what the book is in its Being and is an abecedarian. The poem itself is a prose poem.

Shilly-Shallying Sin purports to be, in the main, a prose sestina that consists of only one sentence.

Abigail Adams and *Belle Boyd* are prose poems of address—i.e., apostrophes.

Coco Chanel and *Dorothy Dix* are collaborative poems. Marianne Moore said that "poetry is not just speech"—hence, it is "a lyric response" in which the "I" speaker reacts to an "other" present in the poem. Kristina Maria Darling notes that: "Even in isolation, one remains in dialogue with shared narratives, cultural symbols, and various ephemera." Mikhail Bakhtin calls this "dialogic consciousness."

Esther is a poem that makes use of appropriation, a kind of excavation which includes passages from Jean Toomer's novel, *Cane.* The epigraph in the poem is a passage that is rendered in reverse.

Fanny Farmer makes use of bracketed passages that use cookery terms and cooking quotes.

Greta Garbo makes use of cinematic terms.

Hypatia is a poem of anaphora—repeated phrases.

Isis is, in part, an appropriation of D. H. Lawrence's story, *A Man Who Died.*

Josephine Jacobsen is a collaboration with Jacobsen's poetry and her text, *The Instant Of Knowing: Lectures, Criticism, and Occasional Prose*, edited by Elizabeth Spires.

Katherine King is a collaborative lyric essay.

Lois Lane is a "riff" using anaphora.

Margaret Mead is a prose poem collaboration.

Trieu Thi Trinh is a prose poem, numeration, and mythology.

Ursula is a collaborative apostrophe.

Valentina Vazzali is a prose poem that makes use of fencing terms.

Wendy Wasserstein is a play.

Xuē Xīnrán is a prose poem that makes use of anaphora and appropriations from Xīnrán's *The Good Women of China*.

Yuko Yamagucchi is a prose ghazal.

Ziyi Zhang is a collaborative prose poem.

A Cronology That Is Not a Chronology but an Account, Autobiography Archive, Biography, Chronicle, Citing, Characterization, Definition, Delegation, Entitling, Fancy, Fact, Grant, History, Investiture, Juggernaut, Kinship, Lagniappe, Ministration, Naming, Ordination, Portrayal, Quest, Reminiscence, Selection, Testimony, Utterance, Verification, Winnowing, Wish, Wisdom, Xenagogy, Yatter, Zest

On a dirt road in Tuscaloosa, red and rutted, a girl turned woman, turned crone wants a name–not the surname of the father who could not, would not marry the mother, for he already had a wife, this carpenter-papa named William, who said it was best to dispense with the child, and hand her off like a sack of new potatoes. The fields were full of them, little nightshades creeping along the ground, and the mother called the newborn "Mary" and in her crowning moment maybe she screamed "*Merde!,*" and maybe she was yelling to the mother of Jesus in her pain, and maybe her child was born in a cotton field, in the broiling sun, in not a lick of shade. The babe had no words then, just yelps and cries and could say nothing about the matter until she reached the roundabout of "was" and "is" and became the crone who would give herself a name, try on identities like dresses, like bonnets, like silk panties she could, at last, afford.

Shilly-Shallying Sin: Like Mother Is an Improper Name

Her body, her mamabody, thick and craving, a house, white bone house on the red-rutted road she never dreamed she would walk down, down past loblolly pines where waiting, she would sometimes braid a bracelet of pinestraw flowers, flowers that would never bloom, those little curly nodes she'd wear on her wrist, her body housing a baby, housing it nine months, but yet unborn, there in the piney woods, backwoods hiding whiskey stills, where that drunkard, that married debt-stud daddy rode her like his mare when she walked into the woods, woods with flowering dogwood and yaupon to meet him, and if the babe is a girl, she will name her "Cassina, Ilex Cassine," or maybe "Holly," and they will walk the red-rutted road together, mother and child, go deep, deep into the forest and play house like she used to do when she was a child living on the country road near Tuscaloosa and together they will name the trees, say "longleaf," "shortleaf," say "pond pines," pines whose very names are familiar friends: "sand pines, pitch pines, slash pines, slash, slash, slashslashslash"–and her wrist, she gentled it, but would she slash it, for it wouldn't matter then, that red-rutted road in front of the run-down house where her own papa lived, where nothing could flower long in his spite-filled house, house she'd leave, and walk, walk away from, farther and farther away, and yet she pines for the father of this child when he says she has to give her baby away, though her mother had already raised a child named "Billie Jean" after her lover's wife's son, child delivered in the House for Unwed Mothers in Birmingham—and now she is pregnant again, but would she slash her wrist and end this flowering, get off this road, road straight to hell, because the preacher said "sins find you out if you don't walk the straight and narrow," that lily-flowered path where pines look up to the heavens as she would do, look to the heavenly house, to the god-house, its wide doors wide open, house beside the gold-paved road where she would surely find Jesus, if only she would turn to Him, turn then, and walk with Him and talk with Him among palisadial pines and corn-stalk flowers and be delivered of sin.

Abigail Adams: We Of Me—Us of Them

Oh, Abigail, Abbie, Diana, First Lady whose epistles I
might have penned   had I believed in
reincarnation,   had I married the second President
of the United States and birthed the nation's sixth
Commander-in-Chief.

An interval greater than a century   blurs
c[h]ronology   my mental calendar blotting,
        obliterating,   the sustaining years
bringing them into a single unit   into a
resounding chiasm   intertwining   binding
we of me   us of them.

Indeed, time is not a father   that old fart
that elderly bearded man, dressed in a   robe
carrying   a scythe.

Time is a mama cat a kangaroo with a pouch
a mother her womb. What matter 1764
1763 1796 1818 2017
quill suspended poised ink blobs
on paper words the measure a counting of
Being's beads male-bag we tote through tectonic
shifts,

but nothing is ever lost you in candlelight
the beam flickering on your page wave upon
wave of it me, here in pre-light
you waking me again at 3:00 a.m. and I think I smell
your apple pan dowdy baking in the oven taste
your gooseberry fool won't you sample my bread
pudding the recipe from the New Orleans
cookbook on my shelf.

The timer is going off maybe not my ears fail me
mondegreen mondegreen and I am a child again
and the preacher in the First Baptist Church of the
Redeemer on Sunday last was talking about
Father Whichart who is in Heaven,

and time is not fleeing; let's say that physicists
which we are not, Abigail neither you nor I
who keep nicking away at it postulating
zeptoseconds and yoctoseconds and
planct time the time it takes light to travel
what could be the shortest slice of cake but time
for you and me is decisions and visions
time for John's figurations your words

when you wrote him to remember the ladies
and be more generous and favorable to them than
your ancestors.

Now I hold your letters in my hand
and read the wit, waft and warrant of your words:
"Too high-sounding," you say.
"Too few actions correspond."

I lament limitations on the rights of women
living centuries after you and take up your
cause. I would write in deoxygenated hemoglobin
and state again over and over again, again
that yes men would be tyrants if they could
and they are and I can't comprehend 650
million years let alone 4.5 billion years let alone
all the years that multiply us by zero,

but I know this I shall hold myself unbound by any
law in which I have no voice or representation.

Words my dear Abbie are our bond.

BELLE BOYD: A SCABBARD ON HER KNEE

"By-the-way, did you ever hear tell of Miss Belle Boyd?"
—from *Belle Boyd In Camp and Prison*

Belle Rebelle, spy, secret agent, propagandist, cross-dresser, glamor-girl, nurse, wife, mother, actress, writer, defender of freedom and champion of motherhood, woman with peeping pistols hiding on the belt around your waist, buttons despoiled from General Shields bold on your breast, you warrant praise while burrs and blurs render an inexplicit cohesion of time and space—your South, "Belle Rebelle," "Siren of the Shenandoah" and certainly mine: the terrain of turpentine and Cotton Queens, of Azalea Maids with pastel hoop-skirts and layers of crinolines. Such panache; we preen and pose as if today were yesterday stitched in lost tomorrows,

the looks that cross—that kill:
eine Art der Reflexion...

I would we could sit, drink sweet tea on the veranda, wile away an afternoon, and read Merleau-Ponty, for indeed, it is in the openness to the world that we rediscover in ourselves and the perception we divine within life that defines us—what you call "the thoughts and intents of the heart, North and South, friend and foe, rebel and loyalist, victim and victor":

phantasmagoria, dream, mirage, masquerade,

your words, yes. Listen Belle, I heard it said you were perfectly insane on the subject of men, heard you took a gun to a drunk soldier and shot him dead for talking to you and your mama in language most foul. Some folks say you had no business mucking about with Yankee soldiers, no matter your intent. "Lord, love a duck," my dear, I hope it's true you hid soldiers under your bed and whispered peace-sighs in their stoppered ears. I hope you ignored the press that called your femininity "hysteria."

Que sais-je?

I understand your sentiments when you say slavery, like all other imperfect forms of society, will have its day, but history claimed you made up the malarkey about camp and prison. Kate Sperry said of all the fools she ever met, you did beat all. Ella Murphy called you "addle-brained." *The Washington Star* wrote of your prominent teeth, your protruding jaw, and manly nose, but

soft you now, fair Belle Rebelle, legend and nymph in your orisons and by all your sins remembered, times change, and it's not 1862. I don't wear a starry band across my brow, don't own a gold palmetto pin to display on my blouse and can't show off a lovely chin, but I, too, can spin a yarn despite truth or consequence. You stand by your verve, vim, ardor, and fire; I'll stand by nouns that define the both of us: belles, balls, buoyance, the scabbard situated across your knees, your derring-do and my balled fist sweet-scented in its velvet glove, my drawl, its precious [a]vowels, as good as a Derringer, some might say.

Coco, La Petite Coco Chanel

"I am not young but I feel young. The day I feel old, I will go to bed and stay there. *J'aime la vie!* I feel that to live is a wonderful thing."

—Coco Chanel

Qui qu'a vie Coco dans l'Trocadéro, donneuse d'eau.

It is past midnight—3:45 a.m. and I have conjured you.

Shall we have a double vichy water on the rocks? And dab perfume wherever we'd be kissed?

You took the 20s by storm, dahling Gabrielle "Coco" Bonheur Chanel; how facinorously you freed women from corsets and doodied them up in menswear. Jackie Kennedy and Marilyn Monroe wore your fancy pants. Why not me?

Just think! Me in jersey trousers. Black. Tuxedo stripe down the side. Me in the fast lane. I'm the metaphor of masculine dreams–that man beside me clad in trousers sort-of brocked beige. His arm's around my waist. He whispers in my ear. I smile. "Summer," he says. He calls me "Summer."

This then: A beach in south Baldwin County, LA.—Lower Alabama. The wind fiddles my trouser legs, riddles my thoughts.

"Wher ah we going?" I croon.

I wear dark glasses with red rims. He removes them, looks into my eyes. And falls. In love.

I grew up in a sand-sexy village near the Gulf of Mexico. Folly. That's not the name of my town—but close. This morning, I'm there by the dunes where I used to park and spoon when I was seventeen, and it was dark and the moon was the only face that peeped through the window. Now condos dot the shore. Luxury hotels have leveled dunes into parking lots and pavements.

Coco, you said "in order to be irreplaceable, one must always be different." Women wear trousers—
luxuriously.

I have an affinity for spies. Didn't realize you were a Nazi agent: FM7124. Code name Westminster.

Anyway, you say "a girl should be two things: classy and fabulous. I don't know why women want things men have when one of the things women have is men."

I just bought your #5 perfume for $99.99 on Amazon. Seems a bit much—

but a girl who doesn't wear fine perfume has no future and can't marry well, marry a Duke or a Brigadier General. Marry a politician. A would-be president of a corporation, maybe a lawyer. Marry a doctor who takes her pulse, his ear pressed to her heart.

Even if you came from the shoddiest stock and were born in a poor house in Saumur and your mama, like mine, wasn't married, it's what you make of yourself that counts. Invention. I'm big on invention.

You say the day you feel old, you'll go to bed and stay there; "*J'aime la vie!* Life is a wonderful thing." And bed is the place that when you go there—he waits to take you in.

I just bought a hat, chroma red, though it needs feathers to swish when I toss my head. Come April, I'm heading for the fair ground race course and slots, home of the Louisiana Derby. Even if it is a cliché, I say one damn horse is not the same as another; one gambol isn't either, and I don't want to be nobody's mare. Still your words are held self-evident: "As soon as you set foot on a yacht, you belong to a man, not to yourself, and you die of boredom."

This morning, naked in the shower, I sang Bessie Smith's "Tain't Nobody's Business If I Do," while warm water poured over me like mercy, like grace, and when I wrapped a towel around my shoulders—so soft, so ready, so reliable, so absolutely there waiting, I thought of how I wasn't bored, not in the least. I'm at the Hotel Monteleone—214 Royal Street. New Orleans. Room... well, never mind. Tonight I'm going to Galatoires for dinner. I'll order soufflé potatoes, poisson meunière almandine, bread pudding, a brandy alexander or two or three until the sun rises over the Big Muddy.

Laissez les bon ton roulet.

You say Coco's a lamentable name, but a name, indeed, is how we fashion it—a little black dress, strand after strand of pearls, a collarless jacket, a well-fitted skirt, a sensational hat, maybe a tie, an Andre Prévin musical composition, and of course, Paris in June.

Dorothea Dix:
Stories Unlaid Stones Might Tell

"The tapestry of history has no point at which you can cut it and leave the design intelligible."

—Dorothea Dix

This then is truth. The Whole Truth—as I remember it—green as unmowed grass, the sharp redolence of burning leaves. Behind our house—an alley. Four houses down were the Gregors. That is not their name; I invented it. Made up the name "Christianna," and I was told not to play with her. Mama said her family was trash. "They don't have a bathroom. They pee in the yard."

My first-grade teacher told Mama I was playing with Christianna at school. She said the girl had head lice.

Mama poked around in my hair to see if I had them too. She went to Stacey's Drug Store and bought Derbac soap as a precaution for the nits I didn't have. "Just in case," she said. "But you may not play with Christianna."

Time and place separate us, Dorothea. You were born in Hampden, Maine. I was born somewhere along the fault line of the Black Warrior River. Your father was alcoholic, my actual father too, that married man who had an affair with my mama. You went to live with your grandma in Boston. You were ten. Your aunt would make a lady of you.

I went to live with the parents who adopted me; I was not yet two—though I, like you, would be refurbished and re-defined. Mrs. Richardson, my singing teacher, said I was a sweet child but had no voice. I tried to throw out my ten-year-old chest and warble *The North Wine Doth Blow.* That's what she said: "Wine." Mama hid wine behind the flour in the cabinet above the stove. No ministers in my family, like yours—but my grandpa, a deacon in the Baptist church, died on World Communion Sunday just as he dropped the collection on the altar. I imagined it sprouted wings, and angels received ready cash in heaven. Mama said my daddy thought dancing was sin, and he quit the day he married her. "I don't have to two-step any more," he said, but before I went to college, Mama signed me up for Arthur Murray lessons, so I'd be sorority material.

My teacher, Joe, fell in love with me; I fell in love with the waltz, not him. I was eighteen. What did you learn from your teacher, Dorothea? Tap? Toe? Ballet?

You gave biscuits and your brand-new clothes to beggars at the gate. You were punished. I ran down the alley, gave Christianna my favorite doll named Annie Kate; she had a hard rubber body but human-like hair. I ran from Daddy, ran down the alley as fast as I could; he took his belt to my legs. I never tripped off to Christianna's again, high-tailing it past the oil barrel where Daddy burned leaves in the back of the house. I was afraid. I'd heard about fire and brimstone on Sundays in the first Baptist Church of the Redeemer.

My now and your then, meet in conjugated verbs in the concreteness of nouns, the stasis of numbers. You were born in April. Me too, your 4th day to my 6th—in a perpetuity of scribbled time. Your reverence of verse, as monumental as my own, rents and wrenches the jaws of words as they try to say the use of their telling:

Alabama Insane Hospital, Tuscaloosa, 1872, Vol. I. *The Meteor*. "Edited by a patient on the 4th of July, a paper for all mankind, whatever their nationality, political principles or religious creed."

The editor wrote that "Miss. D. L. Dix is contemplating a visit to the Superintendent of this hospital. Her numerous friends will be pleased to learn that her health is excellent and that she is still actively engaged in doing good."

I think we're all insane and institutionalized in this land that would be brave and free. We mark our little plots like dogs. We growl. We're trained to fight, and call it justice, call it politics. When I was in college studying education, I took walks on autumn afternoons, walked down the avenue of oaks leading to Bryce Hospital where faces peered out the windows. I'd walk then to unmarked potter's graves and wonder what stories the unlaid stones might tell.

Esther: Strange Words Deep Down

"O way down deep, deep in my ears."
—Jean Toomer' *Cane*

eyes ears evening emptiness
excitation echoes esthergen eeeeeeek

Hair—braided chestnut,
coiled like a lyncher's rope

epor s'rehcnyl a ekil delioc
tuntsehc dediarb—riaH

Mother braids my hair in pigtails and ropes them across my head. Would take more than sheen and a big bow ribbon to make my hair look good. "I'll tell you what," Eloise said. She lived down the street. "You're adopted."

I wanted to know who I was, wanted my straight hair to curl, wanted it to tell, to tell, to tell.

Esther's hair falls, falls in soft curls, falls about her high cheek-boned, boned chalk-white face. It would be beautiful if; if it would be beautiful, there would be more gloss to it.

Barlo, King Barlo, clean-muscled, magnificent black, preaches Jesus, preaches black Jesus, preaches near where Broad came away from Maple Street. Abe, his skin like hardened Elmer's Glue, stands in front of Stacey's Drugs singing "Jesus loves me, loves me, loves. Loves." "jEsUs lOvEs mE, lOvEs mE, lOvEs. LoVeS."

Sixteen: Esther begins to dream—black singed, woolly-tobacco-juice baby, singed black, stained baby—ugly as sin.

White-give-away-baby, hand-me-down war-time baby, baby with Japanese eyes. "She don't look a bit like the parents what adopted her," the townsfolk say. Still, within the year, her parents could take that baby back where they got her, place her once more in foster care. At sixteen, she dreamed of snakes, dreamed she fell in their hissing pits; they swarmed about her, raised their pointed heads, staring with eyes reptilian as her own.

Twenty-two: Esther works behind the counter of her father's grocery store.

I could have poked my nose inside, smelled the snuff, the unguentine, the vagrants lolling about outside, smelled old wounds, scarred over war wounds carrying the rank of memory, the ludicrous stench of loss.

Black folk who drift in call her a sweet-natured, accommodating girl.

I did not fit in with other's wishes. I let Jamie cut my hair, lop it off completely on one side. We can never take back the mistakes that define our life.

Esther recalls an affair with a little fair boy who told her that for sweetness, he preferred a lollypop.

She forgets she's near white, off-white and wonders why she doesn't appeal to men.

Appeal—the peel of skin, the burn, the sun-burn salve didn't cure. I slathered it on.

Appeal—I made love on the beach, on the sand. The waves tickled my toes. "Eat them," I said to him, but he thought they were tasteless, thought I was tasteless, but we waded in the water, the salt of it stinging my skin, scroflulous skin, my starving white scoffled, defiled skin salvaged by memory.

At thirty Esther's hair thins, thin as a thread; it looks like dull silk on puny corn ears. Her face pales until it is the color of the dusk, dark that dances like dead cotton leaves.

My daddy owned a grocery downtown in a place called Folly—a poor investment. Mama said marriage was caviar vs. boiled peanuts; she said it was as easy to marry a rich man as a poor. Sometimes sustenance is not boiled, is not peanuts, is not roe.

Twenty-seven: Mustnt wish. Wishes only make you restless.

Restless love. Frantic love, Love like jazz, the whole note, black note that dies away, just short of a finished song, just short of love, hot like New Orleans in July, like lost bread dipped in batter, grilled and deep fried, the powdered sugar on top mingling with maple syrup, and Old Man River calling , Old Man rivering old worn muddy wishes, like nightmares denying dream.

This aint the place fer you. This aint the place fer you.

Esther and me, dull, puny girls, all ears. We are from flour sack dresses and cotton fields. We are from King Barlo and allochthonous Abe, from lonely corners on shady streets, from drab dawnin' of the morning light, from "shut your ears," from the pages of a book, from where Esther stepped out of the pages of *Cane*, from defining difference and the divisiveness of hair. Esther is black. She was a lil milk-white gal.

My Mammie, she rocked me in the cradle, my Mammie who smelled like butter cream icing. She called me "sugar plum," called me "sugarfoot," nibbled my baby toes; she combed my board-straight hair and kissed me with her brown-sugar lips. I thought she was my mother. I loved her, this mother, mammie, mum, momma, mam, mummy, dam; I loved her long past the day she didn't come to work, didn't come ever again to cuddle me, for my own mother told her to go, told her not to return, fired her for kissing me on my lips with her lips, and I knew then, knew how children know things without never being told, knew the clabber of telling, knew I was not Esther and could never be, but learned what I'd always know from that day to this—that I am poem and story, the land, novel-woman, a crone raisin' Cain.

Hair—braided chestnut,
coiled like a lyncher's rope

epor s'rehcnyl a ekil delioc
tuntsehc dediarb—riaH

(references in italics from Jean Toomer's *Cane*, with variation.)

FANNY FARMER: TRIED AND TESTED

"Progress in civilization has been accompanied by progress in cookery."

—Fanny Farmer

"COOKERY: the art of preparing food for the nourishment of the body."

—*The Boston Cooking-School Cook Book, 1918 edition.*

I've been reading up on cooking, making my own recipe book: "Nothing says loving like something from the oven." Collards simmer on the stove—with fatback and a cookery spoon that clanks and blings. A nip of pot liquor. Maybe, Fanny Farmer, I can be as culinary as you.

"The only real stumbling block is fear of failure. In cooking, you've got to have a what-the-hell attitude.

—Julia Child.]

My *Fanny Farmer* Cookbook rests on the counter-

top, its pages marred by grease, by crayoned drawings my son Jason made more than 30 years ago. He's the gourmet cook, not me, but I need a dessert for Thanksgiving, so I'll try:

Zigaras à la Russse: Make and fry same as Cigarettes à la Prince Henry, using cheese mixture in place of chicken force-meat. Melt two tablespoons butter, add four table-spoons flour, and gradually pour in one-half cup milk, then add one tablespoon heavy cream, one egg yolk, and one-third cup grated cheese. Season with salt and cayenne.

"Sasha had decided she liked cooking. Unfortunately, cooking didn't like her back."

—Naline Singh, *Branded by Fire.*

Cigarettes? Prince Henry? Who the holy hell is he? Google says he's the Prince of Wales, King Edward VII of the United Kingdom. A dish fit for royalty? I don't think it qualifies that I married a Brit who makes pasties and spotted dick, makes tarts, and orange marmalade he eats on toast all through the year. Unfortunately, I set the fat on fire. Almost burned the damn kitchen down. Royalty, indeed!

"He'd noticed that sex bore some resemblance to cookery: it fascinated people, they sometimes bought books full of complicated recipes and interesting pictures, and sometimes when they were really hungry they created vast banquets in their imagination—but at the end of the day they'd settle quite happily for egg and chips. If it was well done and maybe had a slice of tomato."

—Terry Pratchett, *The Fifth Elephant*

I'm a cheese-grits girl, chicken and dumplings, turnip greens and collards girl, and like you, Fanny, I value education in and out of class. I learned a splattering more than Robert and Elizabeth Barrett Browning's poetry from my Victorian professor whose name was Barret though he didn't know a thing about thyme. We thrived on savoring; he took me to eat in fine New Orleans restaurants every week. I learned to relish Retsina, the wine of the gods. "How do I love thee?" he whispered: "Let me count the ways." Ah Retsina—a wood nymph's tears. To hell with force-meat and zigaras. I prefer the puff of poetry to rolling out pastry thin, to cutting it into pieces four inches long and a little more round than a cigarette, brushing it with eggs, rolling it in crumbs, then frying in deep, dangerous fat.

"I want to write the world's worst cookbook. It will feature a *Peanut Butter and Jelly Sandwich* and a *Roasted Roadkill* and *Hitchhiker's Surprise* (this recipe is a secret concoction handed down from my great grandfather to my grandfather, who told it to my dad just before he ran him over.)"

—Jarod Kintz

I understand you're the "Mother of Level Measurements" and say a cupful of flour is measured level like a tablespoonful of cream or a teaspoonful of this or that. Really, I prefer "heaping" and have never been level-headed in my life. I don't like to cook anymore, don't like to schlep up and down the aisles of Publix or Winn Dixie, or stand in check-out lines. I don't know how to tell when a cantaloupe is ripe or an avocado ready for consumption. I do know if you can't stand the heat, you oughta get the hell out of the kitchen—and not just the kitchen either, out of the house—like "sayonara" when husbands aren't worth a hill of beans, but you never married and wouldn't understand.

"Everything tastes better when cooked by someone else."
—Marilyn Taylor Klam

I'm dining out on Thanksgiving. Let someone else stuff the turkey, put giblets in the gravy, and make pumpkin pie. Let them wash the dishes, the pots and pans, clean the counters and mop the floor. Still, if I could cook like you, I might be a chicken and dumpling, a tasty treat.

GRETA GARBO: ZOOM IN

“I like the sea: we understand one another. It is always yearning, sighing for something it cannot have; and so am I.”

—Greta Garbo

[action: the camera is rolling]

Gray and grayer still on long winter nights...

Greta Garbo, nee Greta Gustafasson, you say your father sat in a corner scribbling figures on a newspaper. Poor Father, your ill father, how you took him to the hospital for treatments. Poor father who died when you were just 14.
Poor penurious papa with poverty etched on his brow. Poor streetcleaner, grocer, factory worker father, butcher's assistant father, father with unrealized dreams.

[wipe: a transitional device in which one image slowly replaces another by pushing the other out of the way.]

In the First Baptist Church most Sundays, my father's fingers held one side of the hymnal; my small five-year fingers gripped the opposite side. His voice blended with mine. We sang:

Not the labor of my hands
Can fulfill Thy law's demands;
Could my zeal no respite know...

My zeal to be, to be somebody, and you said, Daddy, you said, I could be a Star.

[banana: Instructing the actor to move in to a scene in a slight arc, or curved path vs. a straight line.]

Father stood on the floor furnace in our dining room, his trouser legs like waving flags. The furnace warmed the front of the house in winter. At night we slept under electric blankets in cold bedrooms with no heat.

[Close-up]

Print like salvation: The Word, word after the word in my father's hands, the now defunct *Mobile Press, U.S. News and World Report, Time, Life,* and *Newsweek*—the world turning in printed pages.

[zoom shot: accomplished with a lens capable of smoothly and continuously changing focal lengths from wide-angle to telephoto (zoom in) to wide angle again.]

[zoom in]

Your mother repaired ragged clothes and sighed.

My mama sat at her Singer, pushing the pedals down up, up down, while the needle played its patient tune, the little drill dispensing thread.

[ad lib: extemporaneously]

I poured over Nancy Drew and Beverly Gray. Read *Lassie Come Home, The Black Stallion*, read to a Cocker Spaniel called Copper who couldn't read.

I read Anne Carson's *Town of Greta Garbo*:

> *When my idol left it broke.*
> *My back it broke my legs it.*
> *Broke clouds in the sky broke.*
> *Sounds I was.*
> *Hearing still hear.*

[Flashback]

Evenings of anxiety, filled with danger in the air. Evenings. Unforgettable evenings for a sensitive girl.

[Bio]

Mama said a man in uniform would knock on the door. "Lights out! Lights out," he'd call. It meant enemy bombers may be lurking nearby. Submarines hiding in Gulf waters.

[Lip Sync (See Dubbing)]

Johnny Mack Brown. I would I could play opposite Johnny Mack Brown, football idol, movie star. Johnny Mack Brown, born Sept. 1, 1904, the very year Henry Ford drove his auto 91.37 m.p.h. and Teddy Roosevelt defeated Alton B. Parker. Johnny Mack Brown, coolest dude in the whole damn town of Dothan, Alabama. Johnny Mack, Pride of Alabama's Crimson Tide, who scored two touchdowns in the 1926 Rose Bowl. And made a grand game-saving tackle in the final seconds.

Fight on, fight on, fight on, men!
Remember the Rose Bowl we'll win then!
Go, roll to victory, Hit your stride,
You're Dixie's football pride, Crimson Tide!

[background]

My mother—the real one who adopted me, said she knew Johnny Mack at the U of A back in her day. She said she had a lead-out with him at a Celebration Ball—even if she wasn't a star—like you in *As You Desire Me.*

[Commentator: A voice (the person speaking may be either seen or unseen) commenting on the action of a film. A commentator, unlike a narrator, provides supposedly unbiased information, maintaining apparent perspective and distance from what occurs on the screen.]

British film critic, Kenneth Tynan said: "When drunk, one sees in other women, what one sees in Garbo sober." The screen is silver lighting Garbo's face, her illumined face, her eyes like stars.

[Jump Cut: An instantaneous cut from one action to another, at first seemingly unrelated, action. Jump cuts will usually call attention to themselves because of the abrupt change in time and / or place.]

I would hide behind a screen, sunscreen, hide my face, my aging face, its lines, wrinkles, splotches. And like Marguerite Duras's, it's ravaged. I inquire about the cost of botox, inquire about filler. The nurse assistant rubs her hands over my cheek, my brow. Up here, she said of my forehead, it's botox. Down here, she moves her fingers around my mouth, it's filler. Costs around $500.00. I was getting a pre-cancerous spot removed from my hand. Insurance covers that—but it doesn't cover vanity, doesn't cover any would-be Greta Garbo enhancements. Sultry and sexy doesn't come in a vial, and GG, I couldn't look like you, even if they put me to sleep and sucked the fat from under my chin, smoothed my neck, and exposed my décolleté.

[Caterer: Responsible for breakfast, lunch, or dinner on a set.]

I cherish ceiling-fan memories—Mama and me sitting on the back porch shelling speckled butterbeans, hearing them clink as they fill the tin pans in our lap. And waiting. Gramma cooked them with fat-back, slow cooked them with andouille sausage, bell peppers, and onions. The taste of heaven in a spoon.

If only I could be a star, if I might kiss John Gilbert. Oh, that pipe in his mouth, oh, his alluring mustache, I imagine falling into his arms, imagine being twenty again or even nineteen, I am "delish," perhaps a Warhol confection, an omelet covered with meringue and set upon a bed of génoise. A gold footed goblet, a pointed pink cone of a hat, a little gold bow on top. An omelet Greta Garbo, girl of your invention as well as mine.

What did you have going with Greta, Andy? Did you pour a glass of beated kirsh and light it, set it aflame. How did you make that bed of genoise?

I see me as a cookie, girl. Am I not a recipe? People search the internet to find how to make me. Eighty Garbo cookies, no less!

Garbo Cookies Hermits Recipe:

1/2 cup butter, softened
1/2 cup shortening
1 cup packed brown sugar
1/3 cup granulated sugar
2 eggs
1 tsp. vanilla
2 1/2 cups all-purpose flour
1 tsp. baking powder
1 tsp. cinnamon
3/4 tsp. each nutmeg and ground allspice
1/2 tsp. ground cardamom
1/2 tsp. baking soda
1/2 tsp. salt
2 cups chopped candied fruit
1 1/2 cups chopped toasted almonds
2 tsp. each grated orange and lemon rind

In a large bowl, beat together butter, shortening, and granulated sugars until light and fluffy; beat in eggs, one at a time. Beat in vanilla. In separate bowl, stir together flour, baking powder, cinnamon, nutmeg, allspice, cardamom, baking soda and salt; stir into butter mixture in two additions. Stir in candied fruit, chopped almonds and zests. Drop by tablespoonfuls, about 2 inches apart on parchment paper or greased cookie sheets.

Bake in 350 (degrees Fahrenheit) oven for about 15 minutes or until golden. Let cool on pans for 5 minutes. Transfer to racks; let cool completely. Store at room temperature for up to 5 days or freeze for up to 2 weeks. Makes around 80 cookies.

[fx (effects) special effects]

Might I be The Temptress, The Divine Woman, The Mysterious Lady, A Woman of Affairs, of Wild Orchids, Inspiration, Romance—by my own design.

[zoom freeze]

"Long winter nights are gray and grayer still..."

HYPATIA: TO RIGHTLY READ THE STARS

"Life is an unfoldment, and the further we travel the more truth we can comprehend."

—Hypatia

I think about dying. According to the Mayan calendar, the world should have ended in 2012 with the rumbles, roars, explosions, crashes, splashes, pops and booms of asteroids sounding our planetary doom. In Alexandria, Egypt where you were born in 370 A.D., Hypatia, daughter of Theon, you made such attainments in literature and science that you are known after more than one-thousand-six-hundred years. You defy time. If I were to walk outside, look up at the stars, might I understand the universe, how we are ourselves the stuff of constellations?

I think about dying. My body feels its aging aches and pains. How many years do I have before me? I view my time in calligraphs on both my hands. Where might I find an astrolabe? Explain, if you will, hydromancy. I believe a water god saved Admiral Farragut as he fought in Mobile Bay, when he cried: "Damn the torpedoes. Full speed ahead."

I think about dying and read my daily horoscope. Today it says that "in order to gain greater insight into what is going on in life, I need to examine another's life choices. But whose? I am an Arian. A ram.

Impulsive. I love without reason. History does not tell the month you were born. If you had rightly read the stars, would you have sallied forth in a chariot the day you died? Might you have known who was waiting to kill you, tear your limbs from your body, set you aflame?

I think about dying, think about my mother; might she have known not to drive to Mobile to see me the afternoon her car veered off the road, dropped into a 50 foot ravine, and crashed into a tree? We had tickets to see the musical, *Singing In the Rain* the evening she would have arrived. A pan of homemade rolls ready for baking and a little suitcase were in the trunk of her car. Her right shoe jammed under the gas pedal. The hospital phoned. Mama was dead.

I think about dying, think about the woman who gave me life before she gave me away. Born on the 12th of July, dead of a heart attack at fifty. Sometimes Hypatia, numbers don't add up, though you were known more for your work in mathematics than in reading stars.

I think about dying—about your death in fourth century Alexandria, notorious for fortune-tellers. Did you, Hypatia, write poems on astrological themes as your father did before you? Did you write a monostich, a one-line haiku, write your own *Peri heimarmenēs*? Does innate intelligence and the power of stars map us from birth until we gasp our last?

I think about dying. Carl Sagan said "we are built of star stuff." Every atom of your body, Hypatia, every atom of mine, the calcium of our bones, the carbon of our genes, the composition of our blood—all derived from a star some 150 billion years ago, and when you died, the star matter in you became the star stuff that lives in me.

Goddess Isis: As Fig-Trees Let Out Leaves From Their Tips

"The goddess in search."
—D. H. Lawrence, *The Man Who Died*

The Search:

And the search—the search for me—me searching faces, searching features. Perhaps I have Isis' eyes and in them see how the lotus blooms. I eye the strand, sit at the foot of a tree overlooking azure water.

Isis in D. H. Lawrence's *The Man Who Died*, searches for Osiris—the dead Osiris whose body is rent, whose arms, legs, the fractured parts, are scattered throughout the world. Maybe his sesamoid bones lie under the catalpa tree in my back yard.

The scent of olives is in the air. How many tunes does the grindstone sing? Its milling drums my ears. Might I be Isis, the "many-named" Isis, the "thousand-named Isis," "Green goddess, Lady of Abundance, woman of invention, of mythology, of Art? I would be a friend to artisans, to sinners, and of the down-trodden as well.

The wind came cold and strong from inland. The sea was invisible, because of the trees, the hum of pines.

Slash pines and long leaf pines chant lexical distortions in the Mobile-Tensaw Delta while tree frogs chorus deep recesses of time. Above is a universe of stars where 4,600 million years ago, the earth was a ball of rock, where once a planet like Mars crashed into earth, where shards of molten debris spun into orbit, and where our little moon shone in Isis's eyes. Moon Goddess, Giver of Life in this stir, this whir of all we would know in our naming, script our fiction, myths, poems, where

olives had given way to pine-trees again—in the darkness, the dreams of the goddess. Isis in search.

Might you help me find myself? I studied mythology in Woods Hall at the University of Alabama where I delved into a search for me, for my Mama, the woman who stood on a street corner waiting for the man who would be my father to pick her up, then waiting to see if he would marry her after I was born. I am myth and mythological, for what, indeed is real? My temple was built of wattles and dreams. Me teaching 12th grade English in a town 236 miles from Tuscaloosa where I was said to be born. And here I was teaching students to parse Love, its gender, number, person, case and syntax...

I did not want his ring on my finger, the fourth finger of my left hand. I gave it back. I wear size eight shoes on clumsy feet; I could never learn to waltz.

Perhaps this is a clue and I can never find myself in you, find myself in a tormented ecstasy of seeking.

If I were a myth, if I were a story, a poem, a line, a simile and maybe iambic, I would never grow old. I would not turn from the mirror where the old woman I see is not me, can't be me, and I turn my back even as I say your name, say Isis,

and the delicate navel of her bud-like belly showed through the asking of her search.

I lost the young woman I used to be, the student at Tulane, the girl wearing white boots and a lavender suede mini skirt. Last time I saw her, she was stepping off the streetcar at St. Charles and Claiborne. She had a book in her hand as she walked toward the levy where good ol boys drank whiskey and rye.

Are all women born to be given to men—open like a flower to the sun of maleness?

I tried men on, yep. I wore their football jerseys, their fedoras, their attitudes. Then I took my husband's name and gave up my own, gave it up like cigarettes, like Retsina, like steak and kidney pie.

O don't go! Stay with me and I will built a house for you and me under the pine trees by the temple...

I want to tell you, Isis, that it is not good to search too long for what may be missing in our life: rooster, python, snake, hard drive, joystick...

(Lines in italics are from D.H. Lawrence's T*he Man Who Died.*)

Josephine Jacobsen: When it was Difficult to Say

"I love the process of being taken from where I am to somewhere else."

—Josephine Jacobsen

If you speak—

in that instant of knowing, in that instant I read *In The Crevice Of Time*, read in *Lines to a Poet*, there in the scissure of your name, a name that might be my name should I adopt it, sounding six syllables, voicing the soft "j," the words and their vibrations travelling air and hiding in fractures of time, in traversals in which I pronounce Josephine Jacobson? But what of us will be acknowledged and what is true in the nor'easters of our knowing?

In Isolation—Identity Indeed—

You are Canada, Ontario, Jo; you are Maryland, Baltimore. I am Alabama, Mobile; we are North and South, the drawl of my tongue, the clip of your Baltimorese, the fronted, dialectical "oh" sound –"eh-ew" or "ao" and that endearing "hon." You say poetry imposes identity.

In the Beginning...in the current of speech...in the inner design of truth, the word, the tongue's saying creates the world—

and it was as if, in the beginning, when a man called Adam gave names to cows: Angus and Africander, Devon and Dexter, Holstein and Guernsey. (My Poppy called his milk cow "Bossy"; at age five I drank her fresh warm milk.) And in the beginning, the man gave names to birds too: "eagle" and "sparrow," "hawk" and "crow," and to insects, ("the dung beetle"), but I do not know words before Babb divided the world and separated names into Swahili, Pashto, Dari, Cajun; your speech patterns and mine.

That word of flesh, like a name, a sound, is what I speak of how my Mama refused to tell my Papa's name, how she was called to court, but would only say she couldn't raise me; she had to give her kid away. And my name came unstuck, my Mama's little doe, gosling, leveret, this contrary Mary she denied, "little bit" Mary, everything Mary of bells and cockle shells. Deleuze and Guttari would call me a nomad that history dismissed, call me an "outsider" in need of a name. Jean-Luc Nancy and François would say I'm a fragment, an essential incompletion that is nonetheless a contradiction.

I drop names, drop the names that fall on deaf ears, me, dropping names on the tip of my tongue, names that taste like turnips, like grits, like peas with bruised, black eyes. Names are nouns, and nouns are words that mean what they do not say, that say what they do not mean, these words I throw out, throw up, aaaargh.

Almost nothing concerns me now but
communication—

and your name, Josephine, a word solid as a child hiding in the crotch of a tree, a child hidden among yellow-orange-russet leaves and flawed blossoms. You must know that the petals of magnolias bruise if touched, and words are blotted and blotched: spots, stigmas, stains, and imperfections. Thanatos is a terrible name, the name "Death" is called; dare we say it? Your father died when you were five. Your mama schooled you until fourteen—and then your name became "muse," became music, became a casting, became a net covering your diaphanous earth.

We can see this—

the way children play, play house, play mother. I wish I may I wish I might know if you played hopscotch on the sidewalk, played "drop the handkerchief?"

Once a girl named Jeanette dropped the kerchief behind me, wild Jeanie, daffy Jeanette who was adopted like me. I stepped on her toes. I am adept at this; been doing it since I was six. No toes are exempt. Your childhood, Jo, shaped the women, the poet, muse, you became: Consultant in Poetry to the Library of Congress, winner of the Marshall Poetry Prize, the Frost Medal, your awards and enviable acclaim.

Presences—

Those bloody-mary verbs I drink, peppery like Worcestershire sauce, with Smirnoff-No.21, and food, like pork belly once relegated to the cabbage pot, but treated now like royalty in trendy restaurants around the world. You're renown, and I would have your fame. William Meredith called you "post-cocious" all those years from 65-85, when you were, with gut and marrow, writing.

The Primer—

Take for example, the animal inside the animal. Say I am cat. And so are you. Maybe I am calico or alley cat, and you're Abyssinian, or Persian. Yes, you say "someone must write a book about names," with a chapter "about the accumulated burden on the bearers of famous names." Our moniker, appellation, denomination, title, tag, designation—what freight, weight, millstone is the label we bear?

We measure as we must—

your monosyllables, my faltering feet, my iambs, heroic verse striving to say the name I'll give myself—when I find it, when I find my frontal bone under a bush or in the gray of a stratocumulous cloud, if I find it like letters in soup, like crab in gumbo, find me a palindrome no less.

(Lines in italics are from Josephine Jacobsen's poetry.)

Katherine King: Glass, Pillow, A Mother's Face

"Her shattered face last lay on a white silk pillow,"
—Sue Brannan Walker

"There then, K, K with a stomach ache. K bent over, K trying to stand straight."
—Koht K

a symbol, a fingernail, K and then K; "KK," the other-than-self K; K, the language of flowers; divination K; "KK," who said "nothing good happens to people who don't go to church on Sunday," K, a certain truth, K in the mirror of my mind, K in my looking glass, K looking over my shoulder, her blood that is not my blood, the hand that bled from the broken glass; Glass K—a text that exists, resists, consists, words worked over illegitimately, illegibly; K a symbol, a proper noun.

K writing the klingen of Klang, this is a thief's journal. Dare I dada dada? *Querelle de Brest*; dare I cut Mama's initials into acacia bark?

Katherine King, M.A. in the Courtauld Institute of Art; Katherine King, General Manager of Marketing and Communications at Yarris Pty Ltd.; Katherine King, in Risk Advisory; Katherine King, Member of WOW, Committee at UGA H.E.R.O.; Katherine King, Reporter at Hearts Connecticut

Media Group; Katherine King, Sustainability Consultant, change facilitator; Katherine King, Biotech Project Manager; Katherine King, Owner of Cosmic Connections and The Galactic Expo; Katherine King, Chef/Owner of Katherine King, Catering Productions; Katherine King, Owner of Red Stick Travel; Katherine King, Assistant United States Attorney at the U.S. Department of Justice, Katherine King, creative all-arounder,

Katherine King, daughter of Ollie Foster King, kin of Steven Collins Foster and his "Old Kentucky Home." You, Katherine, who never thought of Alabama as "home" for the sun shone bright on you in Kentucky, on you in the photograph, image faded-gray of you, standing on the sidewalk where small flowers peeked through concrete cracks, you holding out your pretty skirt, your smile, your eyes as large as joy. Is that a ribbon in your hair, there above a signature that says simply: me? Then there's the two of us, the pair of us, the signature of us through my decision to nominate.

Katherine King, mother who was not my mother but was Mother, the mother, who did not give birth to me, but reared me, endured me, loved me, my mother whose shattered face last lay on a white silk pillow; the cut above her eye still oozed. Leaning over her coffin, I kissed her cheek. It was cold and hard, thin lips painted wrong—the work of an awkward mortician.

Katherine King, if no one knows your name, if you are not in history books, if you are not "LinkedIn," are you nobody? And am I nobody too—me, your daughter, seeking a name she would give herself, a name that would define her as more than a traveling crone, as more than merely mother, as more than an absent grandmother to grandchildren I rarely see, children across the pond, children away from the hugs and kisses of this near-sighted Grandma, worldly Grandma, Grandma who tells stories, this testy woman troubling names.

It is January 1910. A Mumfordville, KY diary on my bedroom shelf bears the name Mary D. King—your Grandmother who writes: "Little Girl came to us this morning. God grant that she may be a great blessing to our home." And another year passes as years are wont to do. And Mary D. writes: Jan 3, 1911: "The year has closed and I have written nothing more in this dear little book, book of joys and sorrows."

Jan 13, 1911, she writes again: "Our precious little baby is one year old today. May many many birthdays come to her, and with the blessings we enjoy today. She is a treasure in our home." Jan 13, 1918. Sunday morning, Mary D. says: "This is our darling's birthday. She is eight years old today. She grows more beautiful as the years go by. She is so happy today—eight little candles on her cake. Miss Weaver her teacher, will take dinner with us. Silver spoon comes to her each year from dear friend of her Mother." April 1933; Mary D says "Many years have passed since I have written in this dear little book. We are now living down among the orange blossoms. Our precious little girl is now Mrs. Brannan. She comes to see us often, but oh how we do miss her in our home. She is dearer to me each day."

In this red book, Kate's mother kept a list of names scribbled at the back: "Alice Volleman, Cantonsville, Maryland - My Old Kentucky Home Committee, Bardstown, KY, Armand Mercell, Los Angeles, Calif; Dr. Cecil Ross, 259 St. Francis St., Mobile"—did he operate on you, Mama, July 10, 1935? You told me you were pregnant, traveling on the train back to Alabama. You said the train jumped the track. You said you lost the baby. Was that the op, Mother? But for that there would be no adopted. Name after name after meaningless name writ by Mary D, name after name in the tattered book with a torn label: "Coffee Canning Jar, Queen City Coffee Company, Hazelnut, Ground, Net Weight 8 oz, West Chester, Ohio 45069."

Katherine King, your own diary, January 1, 1930 to January 1, 1931. Mostly as interesting as a charley horse, those names of guys you dated: Joe and Jack, Charles who was worried because his parents came to see him Sunday, and he was "lit." Aubrey—you danced with him in Fairhope; you went rifle shooting at Orange Beach. Bob Lauder, Buddy, and Bruce and Holley and Horace Campion, and on December 24, a date with Louie, who would be my father one day. All writing, caught in the bang and boff of naming, expropriating.

Katie King. Names blur into somebody who was nobody, into nobody who was somebody, but is anybody somebody if nobody knows her name? Are you nobody? Mamamamamamamamam...

One door, opening into another, door closing, glass door. I can see Katherine King in her yellow kitchen; she stands at the sink washing dishes, hiding the bottle of Mogen David wine she served to her Wednesday bridge club.

Kate King, mother-in-hiding, hiding the truth of my birth. "I will put the information in my safety box." After you died, I held the box in my lap, the tin of it cold to my fingers. When I opened the lid, there was no word of me, who I was, where I came from, me who was not a King like Katherine, nor was she her father's kin, but he, too, took her in and loved her when she thought she was not loved—when her near-sighted eyes began to see noun and verb as one—mother and child, a sentence, pregnant phrases in which I discover myself, give birth to myself, take a goodly name seen through glass—darkly, like love.

Lois Lane: Riff

"Some people spend their ENTIRE lives looking for a way to stand out, to be a person that ANYBODY would call special."

—Lois Lane

At first it was the idea of flying. I was six-going-on-seven, standing in Grandma's back yard, standing underneath a loblolly pine, stretching out my arms, rubbing my feet in the dust—and jumping; I was more than prepared for take-off, prepared to leave the sodden summer rains, the threat of tornadoes, leave Grandpa at his card table playing solitaire. He was a grouch.

At fourteen I wrote long letters to a pen-pal in Britain, a guy who played rugby and had shapely calves. I imagined he could run a million-mile dash.

Maybe he could fly. I was no good at finding the square of the hypotenuse or the shortest distance between here and there. My British math teacher missed his Nottingham home; I let him read my pen-pal's letters. He helped me with my sums; I liked to see him smile.

At fifteen, I imagined being nationally known, nationally revered, a journalist—Lois Lane of *The Daily Planet*. I combed my bangs down on my forehead, bought Revlon lipstick in six shades of red and took a night course in shorthand and typing. I would be a reporter too.

At seventeen, at Gulf Shores, I would park with Jesse alongside sand dunes; I thought he was Superman and believed he could fly. He'd take me in his arms and we would sail above cumulonimbus clouds. I thought of how it would be to marry him.

Superwoman won't grow old. Her face won't fade and accumulate wrinkles. She won't need to slather StriVectin on her brow, her cheeks, her neck at night. She would never be a crone. Could I be a figment of Eliot S. Maggin's imagination?

This morning, at my computer, staring at the screen, my hair isn't combed, my fingernails aren't polished, and I wear lipstick bought from Dollar General. I'm eating Girl Scout chocolate mint cookies and writing verse, a novel about a woman who gave her child away. Lois is the square root of my imagining.

MARGARET MEAD: MEA MEA MEAD

"Women have an important contribution to make."
—Margaret Mead

Margaret, you say "Field Work" and dig in dirt, root out old bones, black ash under your nails, in your nostrils. We keep the dead alive with words; we are each other's kin.

My mama is dead Margaret, as you are dead as I will be dead. You say one life touches another, our living and our dying, and just because bones are no longer housed in skin doesn't mean a body doesn't decohere and determine what living means: composition, conjugation, the "jug jug to dirty ears and other withered stumps of time," those men with their hair tied up in psyche knots, their arms and legs adorned with beaded bands of paraminium nut gum, and the women with their heads shaven and their earlobes distended, their necks and arms decorated with the hair and bones of the dead.

I will take away the "d" in death and add an "r." Say earth. June Goodfield said you were her favorite kind of person, and she couldn't believe you were gone. But what if there were no grieving over your golden grove unleaving and what if you weren't gone at all? What if you are in the fall of rain and with me in New Orleans on a long precipitous afternoon when an hour is not just an hour, and eternity is a drop of water in the palm of my hand? Let's see—oh, say, can you? It is Samoa, 1926, and you tell your sister, Priscilla at age 18 about "the thrills you get from touching the body of another person are just as good and legitimate thrills as those you get at the opera... all mixed up with your ideas of beauty and music and life...you must realize that your body has been given you as an instrument of joy...you should choose most rigorously whose touch may make that instrument thrill and sing a thousand beautiful songs..."

I have removed death's "d," so Margaret Mea, let us sing: "Death Thou Must Die"—Earth, and i.e., i.e., i.e., i.e.; brava, I say "I am because I say, I say myself; I am mea, mea, mea, me."

Nola: Ten Ways to Miss New Orleans

"Our dreams drive us so. One after another. Jasmine sprung bravely from the fertile soil of our suffering. And who can live without dreams? Who loves their brief, sweet passage? *Dum vivimus, vivamus.* While we live, let us live."

—David B. Lentz, *Bourbon Street: The Dreams of Aeneas in Dixie*

1. Count the ways. Some days I feel less than human; maybe it's 2200 BC and I'm a land mass, silt deposited by the Mississippi river. Say Delta. That's me.

2. I'm quite a piece: La Nouvelle-Orléans. 1718. Time is relative.

3. So? I claim I am 29° 57' 53: (29.964722). Or 90° 4'

14” (90.07056) latitude and longitude. I stretch out along Terpisichore, Calliope, Thalia, Mnemosyne in the city care forgot: I am muse. I am NOLA,

4. I’m music. I’m Clarinet—from the family of woodwinds:

> *Way down yonder in New Orleans*
> *In the land of the dreamy scenes*
> *There’s a Garden of Eden...*

I’ve been fingered by the likes of Pete Fountain on Bourbon Street. I’m an arrangement of keys and holes, mouthpiece pressing anxious lips.

5. I call myself Erato, muse of love, of erotic poetry. It is hard to explain how to pick an epithet;

6. I’m the Big Easy, woman of the street; I am Storyville—one line after another.

7. I say whatever pleases me in the name of jouissance, a tart lozenge on my tongue—or the taste of oysters in my mouth, hand-shucked, hand delivered, *laissez bon ton roullette*, and my name’s an acronym, NOLA that conjugates am, are, was, were, shall be.

8. I am Terpsichore, bemused, bemusing, line-dancing. Whoa, who dat? “Who’s dat inside, singin’ who’s dat outside, there between Prytania Street and Coliseum—but who can find Terpischore if they can’t pronounce

the name, but maybe this morning, I'll sit right down and write a letter stating who I am, this mass of me: Dear Ma, Mama, Mommie, Mema, Mum, Mam, Mammy, Mater, mother who called me Mary, leaving me no surname—and so I say what I say

9. names I give myself,

10. beyond all meaning.

Olive Oyl:
More Important Than Dumb Morality

"Well, I'm a woman."

—Olive Oyl

Girlfriend, I found you on-line http://oliveoylloves.com, and in due consideration as to how I might consider your name, pile my hair pointedly atop my head, and ignore the problem of large feet (like a size 8 fits us most comfortably) when it comes to matters of love. It is important to know when a woman reaches a roiling boil, know her smoking point is 375 °F (191 °C). We're talking about bonds and molecules, and things relevant to who we are and the measure of heat.

Women with big feet are said to have more of a sex drive than women with small feet, and men with big feet have large anatomical properties below their belt line. One reason I feel such an affinity for you Ms. Olive lies in my feet. I wore a size 8 shoe when I was a teen. Carson McCullers, too, and she thought if she kept on growing at her present rate, she'd be a freak by the time she was grown. I know a man who said he'd never seen his wife's bare feet until their wedding night; he almost couldn't perform in the proper fashion, he was so turned off by her toes.

I know you met Popeye at the Standard Hotel—lord-a-mercy Olive, I once loved him too, loved those misshapen arms, and I learned to prepare spinach five ways: Parmesan Spinach Cakes served with andouille sausage links, called "hot links" in New Orleans; spinach madeline, gnocci, frittata—and so on.

I imagine you, Olive, propped up in bed against four fluffy pillows reading *The Guide To Pop Culture in Los Angeles*, and I vow I'm going to write *The Guide to Pop Culture in Mobile, Alabama* and *Other Hot Topics Like Love and Pillsbury Biscuits Made From Scratch.*

You never can tell about kinfolks, about pedigree, about who married for the seventh time and the expansion of family—your brother, Caster Oyl, your mama, Nana Oyl, your papa, Cole Oyl. I think this genealogy business is nonsense—who begets who and the question: "who's her daddy, you reckon?" And I've heard more than once about your cousin, Lubry Kent Oyl, and his goings on.

Let me tell you a personal story, Olive. My friend Pat Schneider and I were in Sligo having a seaweed bath—separate tubs, and I had on my favorite earrings—you swinging from one ear and Popeye from the other, and all of a sudden, you took a dive, down into the depths of that spinachy stuff in the tub I was soaking in, and I couldn't find you. Pat got out of her tub—butt naked, and she fished around looking for you. Never found you, girl; you are a slippery one. When I got home Pat sent a gift—you and Popeye, bendable and dependable—but Popeye has taken missing—and I see that big grin on your face like you know something I want to know, and you aren't telling.

Pearl Primus: Liquid Steel

"The dance is a spirit. It turns the body to liquid steel"
—Pearl Primus

There you were Pearl, dancing the Jim Crow Train, jumping straight up in the air, five-feet in the air, when one Sunday morning, a work-weary sister shouted "Jesus knows just how much I can bear," but maybe He didn't 'cause maybe he wouldn't of tolerated it—like even in the 50s when they killed Emmett Till and him just 14, killed him 'cause he chatted up a white woman and maybe called her "Baby," and maybe said he'd been with white gals before, but words have a way of running away, getting loose, getting joogled up, but I didn't know then, didn't know about jiving on a Jim Crow train, didn't know then about Pearl Primus and her dancing.

But Pearl, the dance, that beauty, it claims me too, and the voices don't go away. Did you, Pearl, ever ride a Jim Crow train? Go see your mama on a Jim Crow train—Fisk, Tuskegee, Talladega—on a Jim Crow train? Did you ever see a soldier ride a Jim Crow Train, go out, huntin' freedom on a Jim Crow train?

But you danced the rockin' motion of a Jim Crow train. Jim Crow, crow, crowing; hen and rooster crowing, Jim Crow, Jim Crow, Him Crow Train.

*

Sometimes I think the un-Civil War's still going on. Sometimes I think foul words won't ever die—and you can't take them out and lynch them, those god-awful words, those god-damn words, and you heard them Pearl, heard them shouted at you when you came South with that white husband of yours, and you couldn't piss in a white pot or sop your biscuit with sorghum at Aunt J's Café, or drink a cup of coffee when you undertook fieldwork in Alabama in '44, when the Jim-Crowism you encountered was like a fist that hit you full force in the face.

*

Pearl, take my hand, my four-year old, white hand with its crooked little finger, take it and teach me to dance the Calinda you learned in Trinidad. Teach me to jump beyond any past that confines us. Can you imagine how it must have been in New Orleans in 1819? Imagine that architect, Benjamin Latrobe's face when 500 slaves danced in Congo Square, when they shed their clothes and stripped naked to the thrum of bamboula drums hammering away on a Sunday afternoon? Can't you just see the swaying hips of Vodoo Princess Sanité Déedé undulating like a snake?

*

Dance the Calinda, boo-joom, boo-joom!
Dance the Calinda, boo-joom, boo-joom!
Bamboulabamboulabamoulaboulabam!

*

I'll call you "Mna," Pearl, call you the "Mother who did not born me"; and you'll call me "Little Fast Feet" and you'll sing...you'll sing:

*

The dance
is strong
magic.
The dance
is spirit.
It turns
the body
to liquid steel.
It makes it vibrate
like a guitar.
The body can fly
without wings.
The body can sing
without voice.

The body can sing
without voice.
The dance
is strong
magic:
The dance is life

*

I want my two hands to reach up and embrace overhead, I want to say that whatever else we do as women, as mothers, as daughters, we need to hold ourselves in our own loving arms, make "earth" a verb and dance it, dance the movement of wind, the resilience of pines, the way they move and dance, here in the Mobile-Tensaw Delta, here in Alabama I dare call home.

But Pearl, let me tell you this. I do not know why one human being kills another; I do not know how the world will end, but I do know that while I breathe, while one foot still moves gingerly before the other, I will seek to be what you are to me, a mother who is not my mother,

and I'll hear you croon:

Oh, Mother—
Tell me you love me.
Call me with your soft voice...

QUADESH: NATURE, BEAUTY, SEXUAL JOY

שדֶקָ

If I could speak Arabic, if I could borrow a phone and call on a hot line, if time could stretch across eons as words derive, arrive, contrive, cipher, or compute, I would bid you be my muse. We will drink martinis, eat oysters stewed, nude, and fried, and pour milk into our evening bath. I want a foot massage.

Qadesh, Qedesh, Qetesh, Kadesh, Kedesh, Kadeš and Qades, I have questions concerning pleasure; I have questions about figurations of:

ةوشن
ecstasy

Chemistry joins us. We are wives, lovers, and mothers. It is difficult for me to comprehend any scientific reasoning that might underlie controversial opinions about human pheromones. Clearly the molecular biology is the same across species from microbes to man; can you explain?

There you are, riding the back of a lion, a lotus flower in your hand.

My hands reach out as my painted lips say "lotus," say "blue." There's nothing blue in my garden—and no Monet in my sitting room. Still I say *Nymphaea caerulea*, blue water lily. I say *Nelumbo mucifera* which is pink and of the sun, a crone retooling herself.

Like Odysseus, I know some men leave home and never return. I know women lure them even when the sea is grizzled and gray and colors bedoop and befool beggared eyes.

I would you could teach me comfort in my aging skin, teach me a woman's power, teach me the physics of myself, teach me who I am.

What I know of flowers and flowering, of chickens and coops, is what I know of ecstasy, the scent of heady perfume wafting away. Miss Emily slept with her lover's bones. Miss Amelia's eyes squinched in grief—and eggs? Ovaries run out of them, and this morning, yes, this morning, there are no eggs in the fridge, in the ice box, no hard-boiled eggs, no soft-boiled eggs, no scotch eggs, none to scramble or devil.

Qadesh, are you a state of mind, a recollection—that beach, the boy who lay with me upon it as we were washed in waves? Are you that ecstasy?

REBECCA ROLF: Vivant Pocahontas

"...at least once in our history, there existed the possibility of interracial accommodation. For that one fleeting moment—with the blood-thirsty blades arrested in midair–came a flicker of home that on this continent, at least, there would be no cause to mourn man's inhumanity to man."

—from Frances Mossiker's *Pocahontas: The Life And The Legend*

Ahone

The Great Spirit conceived the moon and stars that shimmer through the night: Mahguahaian, the Great Bear, Plough, Saptarishi—spirit and story.

Amounute

I see you Amounute, look into your eyes, and say it is late April 1607. You are the favorite daughter of Mamanatowic, the great Powhatan chief. You have watched the leaves return eleven times.

I will not count the leaves of my long life. If Papa were alive, he would rake them goodly into a pile—and I, a child again, would jump into the center of them. I remember the smell of burning leaves.

Tassantassuk

They came in swan canoes, the Outsiders. Like giant squirrels, their faces were furry and red, and from their mouth came strange sounds, growls and whines and barks like animals make. They stole Young Deer, took him across the wide water to an island called Kew-ba. Winters passed before they came again, the Coatmen wearing long black robes. This you say you remember, Amounute—the men carrying thunder sticks.

Whe Whe Tassantassuk
Always hungry, always begging
Whew he Tassantassuk
Ya ha ha ne he ho
Y ha ha ne he ho

Today, long past repeated revolutions of the sun, thunder sticks are everywhere. They are hidden under coats and carted into classrooms like Columbine in Colorado, 1999. They are in movie theaters, on the streets of Boston. They are in the hands of campus police, and when a weed-wasted boy shouted naked outside the cop shop on a university campus, a thunder stick shows he will do that no more.

You, Amounute, do not like the thought of
people put to death?

Righcomoughes: Death—To conquer is to live.

Wailing the color of grief, we are, we are not our brothers' keepers. The wounded word wafts through pines and sycamores, through oaks and magnolias, through scrub brush and dunes, and we swarm like insects, war ants, red in the woods.

sawwehone

A girl, blooding-in, becomes the measure of her making. Men without women make trouble, make war.

Arakun

In the ashes of autumn's fire, an old woman tells of Arakun, how he tried to touch everything and grab with reaching hands. At night, he'd steal upon unsuspecting people, come out of the shadows, and frighten them. Mischief thrilled Arakun's heart.

In the dark, an old woman sits by the fire outside her yihacan, her house, sits warming her bones and hears the sound of something she cannot see, hears hisses, whimpers, whinnies and growls. *Kator neheigh mattagh*, she cries. "Truly he is there!"

Arakun, steels his monstrous face, peers with evil eye, and twists his mouth, leering. And the old woman gathers hot ashes and throws them at him. Arakun runs, then, for fear is his own, and he dips his hands in the river, splashes water on his eyes, his nose, his mouth. He screams, and from that day to this, a lesson is learned of what happens when a man goes out looking for trouble.

Shacquohocan

Tawnor neheigh Pocohontas? Is your spirit in the stone I hold in my hand? I found it as I walked this morning, a rock with dark lines. I found it, hard as a dragon's tongue, while a cloud, like floating cotton passed overhead, It is said we must begin with a rock, a tree, a cloud if we would learn to love.

SUSAN SONTAG: SHOULD TRUTH BE TOLD?

"The truth is always something that is told, not something that is known. If there were no speaking or writing, there would be no truth about anything."

—Susan Sontag

A work of art says something. ("What is saying is..." "What X is trying to say What X said is..." etc, etc.). Words alter, words add, words subtract.

"We make an erotics of art"; did I say that or did you? Metaphors mislead even if and even as the soul assumes the form of the body. We read a writer's lips, lisps. Hear. Hear. On my GPS, trying to find my way in New York, I ran into myself in Brooklyn, Park Slope. 373-7th St. Apartment 3 and stayed for just a little while.

I believe I saw Cesare Pavese sitting on the stoop of his virtue. He was writing in his diary and mouthing the words: One does not kill oneself for love of a woman, but because love—any love—reveals us in our nakedness." I thought to throw off my mantle, unsnap my bra and stand there bold before him. I wanted to shout "Love begins in the body." Stating this, however, I know the body poses a problem. I have only one breast.

"Ours is an age which consciously pursues health," you say, "and yet only believes in the reality of sickness. The truths we respect are born of affliction." I thought you were talking to me, Susan, but you weren't. Still I listened in. "Some lives are exemplary, others not; and of exemplary lives there are those which invite us to imitate them."

I lean in close, one ear tuned: "all truth is superficial." Truth? The truth of Simone Weil? Her physical monstrous clumsiness, her migraines, her T.B. But is truth always wanted? Does it smell like collards cooked with fatback? Taste like lettuce in disguise? Health is drinking pot liquor.

We've served our time in sick cells. Flannery O'Connor said she'd never been anywhere but ill though her mama tried to keep the truth of her lupus at bay. Stendhal's mother refused to say "tuberculosis," and Karl Menninger believed "the very word 'cancer' kills some patients who would not have succumbed so fast to the malignancy they suffer."

Novel...a doctor. Trying to keep abreast?

Cure? Obscure? Procure? Insecure? I don't trust barbers, docs, medicos, surgeons with a knife. I don't trust the words they use: Got it all! My breast—a procurement. Cancer doesn't knock at your door before entering. It doesn't ask to come in.

Susan, I did chemo, too. Discourse? 'This cancer... So it's a question of time... Never mind. No matter..."

Is it a virtue in our society to speak of what is not to be named? But look—see the diagram of the rectal-colon? See, the genito-urinary tract ailment of our nation's leaders on the front pages of newspapers. The photograph, can it not say?

It is important to be oneself, but might I be a replica?

Trieu Thi Trinh: An Utterance

"Why should I imitate others, bow my head, stoop over and be a slave? Why resign myself to menial housework?"

— from David B. Marr's *Vietnamese Tradition On Trial*

(Seven or Eight Truths about Trieu Thi Trinh: A Stolen Biography) (After Michael Ondaatje)

Sound Ecology
She could ride a tempest and tame wild waves, wear armor, tunics, and flamboyant shoes, call out in a voice like a temple bell.

Reprisal
A third-century warrior of Vietnam, Trieu would brook no abuse from a man or a woman. She killed her damn-devil's ridin' horse of a sister-in-law.

Utterance
She tied her three-foot breasts behind her shoulders with a thong and rode into battle on an elephant's head, brandishing a sword in each capable hand.

Affirmative Action
She refused to resign herself to the lot of women who bow their heads and become concubines.

Beautiful and Therefore to be Wooed,
Such beauty could shake any man's soul.

These Boots: Made For Walking,
Nine feet tall, she could walk 500 leagues a day.

Animal Therefore I Am: Since Time Therefore Men would rather fight a tiger than battle Trieu Thi Trinh.

Ursula: In the Kingdom of Hearts

"Life's full of tough choices, isn't it?"
—Ursula from *The Little Mermaid*

Ursula, this game and gaming; let's play in the Kingdom of Hearts? Let's say we are mermaids; you're a cecaelian sea witch who helps unfortunate merfolk achieve their goals. I lie on the beach and tan my skin; my body has lured a host of men. Indeed I might compare to Madame Medusa in style and dramatics. Such talent! I warble. I sing:

They weren't kidding when they called me, well, a witch
But you'll find that nowadays
I've mended all my ways
Repented, seen the light, and made a switch
(True? Yes? No?)

I would I could sew—and mend—erase that "d." Ah, Men—capital M. I should tell about Adam lurking in the seaweed trying to spy on me—and I, well...I wrapped my eight arms around him. Call them tentacles if you will; I'm the mother of invention. A man is a man is a man: George Washington, George Bush, Georgie Porgie? And I am pudding; I am pie, the soul of animation, the essence of flair, flamboyance, fabrication, the magic every woman needs to be.

I believe I've run out of calling cards, but you can find me on a summer day boating around Mobile Bay or maybe splashing in the Gulf of Mexico, hanging around with snappers.

"Yeah, I'm an arm full, a lap full. Me Ursula, Ursa, the verser."

Valentina Vezzali: In Tenue

"I'd very happily let you touch me."
— Valentina Vezzali to Silvio Berlusconi

Épée, Fleuret, Rapier, Sabre, Foil, conversation, the play of blades—back and forth, the sound of metal sliding on metal, a fencing match, the engagement as steel contacts steel, *au fer, prise de fer, coulé*, the hilt in your gloved hand.

Valentina Vezalli, I would have long blonde hair with one blue braid like you. I would be Olympian, hang five gold medals around my neck, and name February 14, 1974, my natal day. I would be just old enough, without being a crone in pursuit of what might have been, had I not been a waif.

Picture me in tenue, in whites, as I parry, blade down and pass. *En Garde*: Every woman should know how to fence, be on the fence like a Republican, a Democrat, a member of Congress or the Italian parliament—but keep the face covered—*volto coperto*; wear a mask and hide unwelcome tears. Your mother called your blue eyes "two little pieces of heaven that she herself had stolen."

Words foil and fail me, for they cannot erase lines that menace my face. Even if I might extend an arm and blade and counter aging, there is no redoublement, no reprise for the agglomeration of years, but I shall show my mettle and raise awareness of issues concerning people of modest means, and maybe I will dance under a canopy of stars on Dauphin Island as if I were 19 once more.

Wendy Wasserstein: If Only

"I am" became an ongoing question: "Who am I?"
—Julie Salamon, *Wendy And The Lost Boys*

I don't know why I'm telling you this, Wendy. I never rode the D train or lived in Brooklyn, and I am not Susie Friend with pink yarn hair. I don't own a pink sweater or Weejuns, but I am an uncommon woman trying to figure out how it means to live.

My husband says I'm good at scenes—domestic and otherwise—and I can create them in a moment's notice, stage them in a flash.

There—in the wings—a long shadow. The sound of laughter holds the theater in thrall. The shadow can never contain its body, but let us say the shadow is "Ren," the name given to a baby at birth: Wendy. Wendy Wasserstein, Wendy Darling, Sweetsie-bud, Wendee, Wendella, Monkey. And as long as your name is spoken, you are there—wherever there may be.

Set. Set-up. Song: "Anything Goes": Play in the process of prose, in the perambulations of poem.

A bare stage with two beds separated by a veil of gauze, a veil of collapsible time. Two women stir in their berths. The woman on the left is lost in yesterday. She peers under her four-poster bed. The other woman, younger by 11 years, is eating wiener-schnitzel and dumplings with a silver spoon: shiksa, plump, cherubic, and seemingly shy, she reaches to the bed-stand, grabs a cup, and swills tea. The two women are Girls, capital G. Together they sing:

Girls, girls, girls
Long legs and burgundy lips
Girls, girls, girls...

Scene 1:
Legend on the screen: Secrets Aren't Secrets Anymore

Girl 1: (In a nightgown, reaching under her bed) "You can come out now. The war's over. The peace treaty's signed, and if you can help me out of this bed, we can run out on the street together—me, brave belle, and you the soldier I hid before they ran me out of town. Time is the shortest distance, isn't it? I mean, on-stage, the mirror of ourselves in décolleté. A thought-experiment come to life, essential anatomy. First, can I fix you some grits? Bacon? Eggs?"

Girl 2: "Survival lies—or is it lays? Never could do grammar good. So survival lies in hiding truth? If you don't talk about it, it doesn't exist; it's the absence of color, the looking glass we hold to see what can't be seen except in mirrors."

Girl 1: "I wrote a couple of plays once, you know? *The Light Guitar* about Octavia LeVert, Yankee lover, spy, traitor. Edgar Allan Poe wrote her a love poem. If I'd been in New York, Brooklyn, something might have come of my lines. 'If only' doesn't exist, and I was a secret."

Girl 2: "Without children there is no hereafter. On August 17, 1999, I was forty-eight years old and six months pregnant. I named her Lucy Jane. She weighed 1 pound, 12 ounces, shoulders like Audrey Hepburn in a white strapless Cecil Beaton gown. The nurses call me 'Mommy,' told me to attach two plastic bottles to my Hindenburg-sized breast. 'Pump,' they said. Every three hours. Pump. Pump. Pumppumppump. And take the milk up to NICU and put it in the fridge."

Lucy-in-the-Sky With Diamonds. The father? You would ask, but that's a secret!

Scene 2:
Legend on the Screen: They Say My Play Has Too Many Scenes.

Girl 1: "Do you think we could go out for callaloo and salt fish? Lunch at Luchows near Union Square?"

Girl 2: "And listen to the music of an oompahband? We are what we eat."

Girl 1: "Would you believe—when I found my siblings, Jean and Walter, Lil and Larry—they'd never heard of me. Their mother, I mean—my mother—our mother

—never told about me. They staged a 'New Union,' August 24, 2002. My brother said it couldn't be a RE-Union since they'd never met me. Gave me a Certificate of Re-Adoption—joined me up again with my birth family, with all the privileges and affection warranted this new berth. My birth. Time wrings its hands and lies. Secrets. Secrets. Regrets."

Girl 2: "They sent Abner away. Abner and sister Sandra had different fathers from Georgette who learned her Uncle George was Mother's first husband. Nature nurtures us."

Girl 1: "And I have crept into your play, Wendy. Let's call it 'The Summer of What Was, The Winter of Nevermore'. And when you died of lymphoma, they dimmed all the lights on Broadway."

Girl 2: "Against all odds, we hold the gnarled hands of time."

Xue Xiran: Mother-Longing 薛欣然

"But in so many ways my book was my life. It was my testimony..."

—Xue Xiran in *The Good Women of China*

Girls Wanting Mothers

give   give us   give us this   give us
this day   our stories   give us herstory
(re)membering   "a daughter spent every day
longing for her mother"   give us "images im-
possible to reconcile"   "she walked out of
Stanford Brook tube station on a dark autumnal
night"   the sound of rushing   footsteps   how she
fell   fell then to the ground   her body crum-
bling   how she clutched her handbag   "invisible
hands"   and "passersby" shouting   "the salty
taste of blood in her mouth" and "later the policeman
asked why she had risked her life for a bag"   black bag
pharmacon   bag with a book inside
"testimony"   her book   her life   the thoughts
of Chinese women "the good women of China"
"when you walk into your memories"   "when you open
a door to the past"   when you give
          give us "the girl who kept a fly as a pet"
"the scavenger woman"   "the mothers who
endured an earthquake"   the woman who waited
"the woman whose father did not know her"
the woman who never knew her father

who never knew her mother Xinran "It is as if
a pen stabs the heart" for woman's sake

she kept kept that " baby fly as a pet"
"the feet of a fly felt soft and gentle" playing
her cheeks it did not near her lips "did not kiss
her" its red eyes its five eyes peering in her begotten
eyes it never grew up, the fly. she didn't
want to but did grow up.

she kept herself kept to herself "neater than
other scavenger women" "she earned 400 yuan
a month selling scraps" selling giving herself
away

she kept wiping her eyes her dry eyes
heard "nearly every day at dawn," "heard a train
rumbling," again "cries of children" the cries
whimpers always there always in
the cries she would tell her daughter's story
again "some people say the earthquake was ret-
ribution" walls collapsing rubble revenge
"it is mine sayeth the Lord" and "yes, you must
have heard how much destruction an earthquake
causes" like a hurricane a tsunami and the
mothers that time failed to heal

he kept searching "searching for her
husband" time is not the shortest distance
"during the nightmare" "the Chinese Cultural
Revolution" the duration "forty-five years

of yearning"   "so many wrongs committed"
"women are water"   "men are mountains"

" each sentence" writ in watery ink   she kept
speaking the names her mother gave her;   names like
poetry;   "Shu (tree)"   "Shi (rock)"
words caught in limbs of trees

she kept fingering the bag   black bag thick
like medicine   kept reaching   drawing out
scraps   she would pass   like bread
breaking it then   touching it to her lips   taking it
in   story after story   tongued   like tolling bells
to give   to give away   this day   the bread
blessing   the lives   of us   of Xīnrán 薛欣然,
of girls given away.

YUKO YAMAGUCHI: A SHELL HELD TO THE LISTENING EAR

"I never let myself worry about what other people will think."

— Yuko Yamaguchi

Please draw us, Yuko Yamaguchi, draw my sister and me together. Draw us, with you, in Yama-nabe style and sign the picture 緒に, say *issho ni*: together. Draw us as clouds in Kobe, as aspen trees in Saskatoon, as thunder in Alabama. We are the heartbeat of each other's dreams if we're together. Draw us in a stroke of love's listening—and let us hold a shell to our ear, hear the whispers of girls drawn together. Sit at your kitchen table Yuka, colored pencils in a cup at your right hand. We will celebrate the Nagashibina, dolls dressed in bright kimonos, dancing together. Float us in a double-ender boat down the Black Warrior River, float us to the River Styx, to the Gulf of Mexico as we drift along together. Keep us from a fisherman's net; erase predators lurking in the water. Draw our boat docked on colored sands and let us discover womanhood together. Sketch Billy Jean in teal, in Kanju, like this: 慈音. Write Sue in crimson: 寿. We're the possible of pencils; sisters together.

Ziyi Zhang: To Renounce Restraint

"I don't care if you love me or not, I'll love you anyway."
— Ziyi Zhang

Běifāng de shūn, Lady of the North, lady of Beijing, lady of Sheep Year 1979, lady of passion, lady who wanted everyone to live together, you, bird-lady, swallow-lady, crouching tiger lady, lady knocking on wall of the Rouyuan Gate; let me in.

Kids are playing in the yard, playing with the dog, the boys playing soccer or chase, the girls doing the peacock dance, displaying plumage, each one stunning and singular, children whose lithe bodies lust after freedom and renounce restraint.

In 10th grade, my friends and I played hooky from school, cut Spanish class, and drove Becky's pink and black Model A to the Gulf, sang Elvis songs—*Love Me Tender*, and *Heart Break Hotel*, and dreamed of suitors who would love us beyond eternity. But you, Ziyi, said such a dream doesn't happen, didn't happen to you, and you ran away from school at age 13, hid in a thicket of grass and went to sleep.

When we awaken, we are no longer "Little Girls Blue." The sheep's not baaing baaing in the meadow and the cow's not mooing in the corn, but the horn is blowing and we're leaping hedge-rows and dancing out of confinement, our free full-feathered selves ready to fly.

Conversities

(After Marianne Moore. The story in which a woman is assembled, reassembled, and affirmed.)

Abigail Adams (November 22, 1744–October 28, 1818) was the wife of the second President of the United States, John Adams, and mother of the sixth President of the United States, John Quincy Adams. Abigail Adams's life is remembered in the letters she wrote to her husband while he worked with the Continental Congress to create documents that would establish the United States and its government. John Adams consulted his wife on many occasions, discussing intellectual quandaries about political or governmental issues. Her letters serve as eyewitness accounts of the American Revolutionary War. Assuredly, then, she said: "If we mean to have heroes, statesmen, and philosophers, we should have learned women."

Belle Boyd (May 13, 1843–June 11, 1900) namely, Isabella Marie Boyd was a spy for the Confederate Army during the American Civil War and known as "Cleopatra of the Secession." She was born in Martinburg, West Virginia to Benjamin Reed and Mary Rebecca Boyd. Her career as a spy for the Confederacy began after an incident in which she shot and killed a Union army soldier for insulting her mother. At Front

Royal, when her skirt was shot full of holes, she greeted General Stonewall Jackson and his men's arrival to the front. After the war, she toured the country, retelling dramatic stories of her role as a spy in the Civil War. Boldly, she said: "There are those who maintain that in this world women have no right to interfere in the affairs of state, in politics, in plots and counter-plots. Others that are...more chivalrous, are willing to admit that women have as much right to act, think, and speak as men."

Coco Chanel, nee Gabrielle Bonheur Chanel (January 10, 1883–January 10, 1971) is the daughter of Albert and Eugenie Chanel of Saumur, France. Coco was a French fashion designer and founder of the Chanel brand name. She is best known for her role in liberating and modernizing women's fashions after World War I, by creating casual, chic clothing that did not require corsets. A woman of prudence, determination, and ambition, Coco Chanel was a successful business entrepreneur in a then male-dominated field. She was a notable figure of controversy as well, especially in World War II, during the German occupation of France where she was said to have assisted the Nazis. Cool, coquettishly, certainly, she knew "women have always been the strong ones" and oh, yes, must "dress like you are going to meet your worst enemy today."

Dorothea Dix (April 12, 1802–July 17, 1887) was born in Hamden, Maine, the daughter of Joseph Dix and Mary Bigelow Dix. A chief advocate of humanitarian reform in American mental hospital institutions during the nineteenth century, her work included prison reform, instruction for the mentally challenged, and educational training for nurses. She toured Alabama in the 1840s and was instrumental in hiring Peter Bryce as the first Superintendent of the Alabama Insane Hospital (later Bryce Hospital). Louisa Dorothea Dix determined that: "Society, during the last hundred years, has been alternately perplexed and encouraged, respecting the two great questions: how shall the criminal and pauper be disposed of, in order to reduce crime and reform the criminal on the one hand, and, on the other, to diminish pauperism and restore the pauper to useful citizenship?" [Remarks on Prisons and Prison Discipline in the United States]

Esther came into the world in 1923, as the fictional brain child of Jean Toomer (December 26, 1894–March 30, 1967), author of *Cane*. In the "Afterwords" to *Cane*, Toomer writes that "the act of naming and self-definition would remain an obsession with him. Ears, eyes, emptiness;" Esther says "I'll not think. Not wish."

Fanny Farmer (March 23, 1857–January 15, 1915) is the eldest of four daughters born to John Franklin Farmer, an editor and printer, and Mary Watson Merritt. Turning disability into capability, Fanny recovered from a paralytic stroke when she was 16, and though crippled, she went on to enroll in the Boston Cooking School at age 30 and excel in domestic science. She is the author of the famed *Boston Cooking School Cookbook*, first published in 1896. The book was initially published at Farmer's expense. She said, furthermore, "I certainly feel that the time is not far distant when a knowledge of the principles of diet will be an essential part of one's education. Then mankind will eat to live, be able to do better mental and physical work and disease will be less frequent."

Greta Lovisa Gustafsson Garbo (September 18 1905–April 15, 1990), nicknamed "The Face," was the daughter of Anna Lovisa Karlsson and Karl Alfred Gustafsson who died when Greta was 14. The family was impoverished and lived in what was considered the slums of Stockholm. Greta did not attend high school and first worked in a barbershop as a soap-lather girl. She later worked in a department store where she became a fashion model. She was subsequently discovered by the Swedish film director Mauritz Stiller, travelled with him to America, and became a preeminent movie star. *The Guiness Book of World* Records called her "the most beautiful woman who ever lived." She never married and once said, "I live like a monk: with one toothbrush, one cake of soap, and a pot of cream." Glibly, then, she said: "Life would be so wonderful if we only knew what to do with it."

Hypatia (c. AD 350–415) was the daughter of Theon Alexandricus. A mathematician and philosopher like her father, Hypatia became the Head of the Platonist school where she gave instructions regarding Plato's philosophy. The *Byzantine Suda Encyclopaedia* noted that she remained a virgin and once rejected a suitor with her menstrual rags, saying that they showed there was nothing beautiful about carnal desire. The American literary critic, Stephen Greenblatt claims that Hypatia's murder marked the end of Alexandrian intellectual life. The 2009 movie, *Agora*, portrayed Hypatia's final years. Hectically, she said that "in fact, man will fight for a superstition quite as quickly as for a living truth—often more so, since a superstition is so intangible you cannot get at it to refute it, but truth is a point of view, and so is changeable."

Isis, a goddess from the polytheistic pantheon of Egypt. She was worshipped as the ideal mother and wife and was considered the patroness of nature and magic. She was the friend of slaves, sinners, artisans, and the downtrodden though she also heard the prayers of wealthy maidens, aristocrats and rulers. As the mother of Horus, the falcon-headed god, she was associated with the king and with kinship, and was also known as the goddess of children and the protector of the dead. She married her brother, Osiris, and conceived Horus with him. She speaks forever through the pen of D. H. Lawrence in an erasure of "Shades": an Iteration.

Shall I tell you, then, how it is?—
There came a cloven gleam
Like a tongue of darkened flame
To flicker in me.

And so I seem
To have you still the same
In one world with me

In the flicker of a flower,
In a worm that is blind, yet thrives,
In a mouse that pauses to listen

Our darkness: do you understand?

Glimmers our
Shadow; yet it deprives
Them none of their glisten.

In every shaken morsel
I see our shadow tremble
As if it rippled from out of us hand in hand.

As if it were part and parcel,
One shadow, and we need not dissemble
Our darkness: do you understand?

For I have told you plainly how it is.

Josephine Jacobsen (August 19, 1908–July 9, 2003) was a Canadian-born, American poet, short story writer, and critic. She was the 21st Poet Laureate Consultant in Poetry to the Library of Congress in 1971. Her awards include the Hoover and the Robert Frost Medals. She was referred to as the nation's "Grand Woman of Letters," and said judiciously: "Poetry is like walking along a little, tiny, narrow ridge up on a precipice. I think poetry is dangerous. There's nothing mild and predictable about poetry."

Katherine King (January 13, 1914–November 11, 1989) was born in Kentucky but lived most of her life in Foley, Alabama. She was the daughter of Ollie Foster King, kin of the musician Stephen Foster and Mary Lansdale of Kentucky. She was the wife of Louie Wesley Brannan, a good wife and devoted mother who wanted her child to be someone someday. "Karma," she'd say. "Mind what you do."

Lois Lane created by writer Jerry Siegel and artist, Joe Shuster in Action Comics #1 (June 1938) was an award-winning journalist and Superman's Girl Friend in Issue #80 (January, 1968). When Superman proposes and Lois accepts, they became man and wife in the December 1996 special "Superman: The Wedding Album." Lois was featured in the 1966 Broadway Musical "It's A Bird, It's a Superman," and she said luxuriously: "Tomorrow night, they're going to give me the Pulitzer, but there are a dozen other stories out there; I spent the night with Superman."

Margaret Mead (December 16, 1902–November 15, 1978) was the daughter of Edward Sherwood Mead, a professor of finance and Emily née Mead, a sociologist. She studied at Columbia University and received both an M.A. and a Ph.D. degree. As an anthropologist, she carried out field studies in the Pacific and is well known for her book *Coming of Age in Samoa* (1928) and for significant statements she uttered so meaningfully: "Our first and most pressing problem is how to do away with warfare as a method of solving conflicts between national groups within a society who have different views about how society is to run."

NOLA aka N'Awlins, Hoboken near the Gulf of Mexico, Crescent City, city that care forgot, place and person: we are where we are –saying then and now, "we're a gumbo. We get focused on the very simple notion that diversity is a strength; it's not a weakness."

Olive Oyl was spawned by Elzie Crisler Segar in 1919 and later became famous as a cartoon. Olive's father is Cole Oyl; her mother is Nana Oyl (think "banana oil" – an expression kin to "horsefeathers." She comes from an extensive and notable family. Her brother is Castor Oyl; his estranged wife is Cylinde Oyl. Olive's nieces are Diesel Oyl and Violet Oyl and her two uncles are Otto Oyl and the intrepid explorer, Lybry Kent Oyl. Standard Oyl, a distant relative, is a wealthy corporate magnate. Olive is a sort-of surrogate mother to the foundling Sweetpea. Before meeting and falling for Popeye, she was the fiancée of Harold Hamgravy, but later told Popeye: "Oh, you take your hooks offa me or I'll lay ya in a scupper."

Pearl Primus (November 29, 1919–October 29, 1994) was a dancer, choreographer, and anthropologist known to be a pioneer of African dance in the United States. She received an M.A. and a Ph.D. at New York University. President H. W. Bush awarded Primus the National Medal of Arts. In addition to her many accomplishments, she did anthropological field work in Alabama, and said about prejudice: "Dance is my medicine. It's the scream which eases for a while the terrible frustration common to all human beings who because of race, creed, or color, are 'invisible.'"

Qadesh (aka Qedesh, Qetesh, Qudshu) was originally a Semitic deity whose worship was prominent in Egypt during the New Kingdom, (1570–1293 B.C.). She is known as the Egyptian goddess of love and sexual ecstasy. Her husband is said to have been the Syrian deity, Reshep, ca, 2040–1640 B.C. A woman of quality, Qadesh is, according to the NAS Old Testament Hebrew Lexicon, considered sacred.

Rebecca Rolfe (Pocahontas, c 1596-1617) was known as Amonute, the daughter of the Indian Chief, Powhatan. She is said to have saved the life of Captain, John Smith. In 1615, she married the tobacco planter, John Rolfe and bore him a son, Thomas Rolfe. It is reported that Rebecca, your father valued you less than old swords, pieces, and axes.

Susan Sontag (January 16, 1933–December 28, 2004) was a critical essayist, cultural analyst, a novelist and a filmmaker. She is, perhaps, best known for *On Photography* and *Illness as Metaphor*. She was born in New York City, pursued graduate work at Harvard and abroad in Europe. In 1964, she received recognition for her essay "Notes on Camp." She was also known for her nonfiction works such as *Against Interpretation and Other Essays* (1966,) and for her novels, T*he Volcano Lover* (1992) and *In America* (2000), for which she won the National Book Award. Yes, Susan, silence "remains, inescapably, a form of speech," and yes, "existence is no more than the precarious attainment of relevance in an intensely mobile flux of past, present, and future."

Trieu Thi Trinh, also called Lady Trieu (Bà Triệu) or Triệu Ẩu (趙嫗), was born in a small village in Vietnam. She was orphaned as a toddler and lived with her brother. When she saw that her people were oppressed by the Chinese, she established an army base and began training a thousand rebels to fight. Before age 21, she fought over 30 successful battles against the Chinese with her rebel army. She was said to be over nine feet tall with a voice that sounded like a temple bell. She rode into battle on an elephant, wore gold armor and carried a sword in each hand. In 245 CE, the Chinese won against Trinh. In her despair, she is said to have committed suicide by throwing herself into a river. Today she is a national hero in Vietnam and honored by a national holiday. Women remember words she told her brother as lasting truth: "I will not resign myself to the lot of women who bow their heads and become concubines. I wish to ride the tempest, tame the waves, kill the sharks. I have no desire to take abuse."

Ursula is the main villain in the Disney animated movie "The Little Mermaid." She is a witch with the lower body of an octopus.

Valentina Vassali (February 14, 1974) is an Italian fencer, and politician. As fencer she has won six Olympic gold medals in foil competitions and is one of only four athletes in the history of the Summer Olympic games to have won five medals in the same individual event. In 2013, she entered into politics and became a member of the Italian Chamber of Deputies. In sports, Vassali says to respect your opponent, but in terms of politics, she gives her point of view, that "if all politicians were a bit more sporty, every country in the world would be better off."

Wendy Wasserstein was born Oct 18, 1950 and died from leukemia on June 30, 2006. She was an American playwright and the Andrew Dickson White Professor-at-Large at Cornell University. She received the Tony Award for Best Play and the Pulitzer Prize for Drama in 1989 for her play, *The Heidi Chronicles*. Whereupon Wendy said: "The trick is to find the balance between the bright colors of humor and the serious issues of identity, self-loathing, and the possibility for intimacy and love when it seems no long possible or, sadder yet, no longer necessary."

Xuē Xīnrán 薛欣然, born in 1958 in Beijing, China is a British-Chinese journalist, author, speaker, and advocate for women's issues. From 1989 to 1997, she had a popular radio program called "Words on the Night Breeze." Many of her books consist of interviews that convey the thoughts, and experiences during and after the Chinese Cultural Revolution when Mao and communism ruled. Many of her books: *The Good Women of China* (2002), *What The Chinese Don't East* (from her columns in *The Guardian*, 2006), and *China Witnesses: Voices from a Silent Generation* based on 20 years of interviews (2008) might be called guidebooks or xenagogies. Xuē Xīnrán says "memories keep coming back. Reading, sharing, and thinking can help us find out who we are and what we want from our lifetime."

Yūko Yamaguchi was born on October 21 in Kōchi, Japan. She is the Japanese character designer and illustrator of "Hello Kitty." "Kitty" is a cute (emphasis on cute) anthropomorphic white Japanese Bobtail cat with a red bow on her head. The striking thing about "Kitty" is the fact she doesn't have a mouth. When

Yamaguchi was asked about this, she said yarely, "Kitty doesn't have a mouth so people who look at her can project their own feelings onto her face."

Ziyi Zang was born in Beijing, China on February 9, 1979. She is a film actress best known for her role in *Crouching Tiger, Hidden Dragon*, *Rush Hour 2*, and *Memoirs of a Geisha.* Not just a beautiful face, she pursued her acting career zealously and said she enjoyed being an actress because it enabled her to feel different women's lives. "I have the chance to feel like a geisha one day and on another day maybe a scientist. That's the interesting part for me. My profession helped me grow up."

Afterword

"However...
I have walked through many lives,
some of them my own,
and I am not who I was..."
—Stanley Kunitz, *The Layers*

"I was I was not who was not was not who."
—William Faulkner, *The Sound and the Fury*

www.ingramcontent.com/pod-product-compliance
Lightning Source LLC
Chambersburg PA
CBHW020358170426
43200CB00005B/221
* 9 7 8 1 9 4 2 9 5 4 4 6 0 *